A peek inside the therapy room:

Exploring the journey from both sides of the couch.

By

Joyce O. Muirhead

Disclaimer

copyright ©2023 Joyce O. Muirhead All right reserved.

Preview

A Peek Inside the Therapy Room: Exploring the Journey from Both Sides of the Couch" is a comprehensive and engaging guide that provides readers with a deep dive into the world of therapy. This book aims to break down the stigma and myths surrounding therapy, and offer an inspiring and educational look at the therapeutic process from both the therapist's and patient's perspectives.

The author, an experienced therapist, invites readers to step inside the therapy room and experience what it's like to be on both sides of the couch. Through a series of real-life examples and vivid descriptions, the author provides a behind-the-scenes look at the therapy process and what happens during a typical session. From the initial intake to the therapeutic relationship, the author provides an in-depth understanding of the various approaches used by therapists to help individuals overcome their challenges and achieve their goals.

In addition to the therapeutic process, the book also provides practical tips for those considering therapy for the first time. It covers the various factors to consider when choosing a therapist, such as their training, experience, and therapeutic style, as well as tips for making the most of your therapy experience. The author also offers guidance on how to prepare for your first therapy session, including what to expect and how to get the most out of the experience.

This book is a must-read for anyone interested in learning more about therapy and the healing journey. With its engaging narrative and insightful perspectives, "A Peek Inside the Therapy Room" is a guide that will empower and inspire readers to take control of their mental health and seek the help they need to achieve their full potential. Whether you are a seasoned therapy-goer or just starting your journey, this book will provide you with a new appreciation for the transformative power of the therapy room.

A peek inside the therapy room: Exploring the journey from both sides of the couch.

Therapy is a process that can be beneficial for both the therapist and the patient. It can be a powerful tool for helping people understand and manage their issues and can help them to develop healthier coping skills.

The patient's perspective

The patient's perspective in therapy is one of openness and exploration. The patient is encouraged to be honest and open about their thoughts, feelings, and experiences in order to gain insight into their emotional and mental states. This can be a complicated process, as it requires the patient to confront and analyze issues that may be difficult to accept or talk about.

The therapist's perspective

The therapist's perspective in therapy is one of support and guidance. The therapist strives to create a safe, non-judgmental environment for patients to explore their thoughts and feelings. They provide a listening ear, offer insight and advice, and help the patient make connections between their behaviour and emotions. The therapist also works with the patient to identify and develop strategies for achieving those goals.

Finding the right therapist

Finding the right therapist is essential for successful therapy. It is crucial to find someone that the patient feels comfortable talking to and who they can trust. It is also necessary to find a therapist specializing in the patient's specific issue, as this will ensure they get the best possible treatment. Additionally, it is beneficial to ask for referrals from friends, family, and healthcare providers in order to find a qualified therapist.

Types of therapy

There are many different types of therapy, such as Cognitive behavioral therapy, dialectical behavior therapy, psychodynamic therapy, and family therapy. Each type of therapy has its own approach and techniques, so it is essential to research different kinds of therapy to find the one that best suits the patient's needs. Additionally, some therapists may use a combination of different types of therapy in order to provide the most comprehensive treatment

. Cognitive behavioral therapy focuses on teaching the patient new skills to manage their thoughts and behaviors. Psychodynamic therapy looks at the underlying causes of a patient's issues, while family therapy focuses on resolving issues within the family unit. Dialectical behavior therapy is a form of cognitive behavioral therapy that focuses on teaching patients how to regulate their emotions.

The benefits of therapy

Therapy can provide a wide range of benefits, including improved self-awareness, stress reduction, and improved communication skills. Additionally, therapy can help individuals process difficult emotions, manage overwhelming feelings, find healthier ways to cope with life challenges, and build better relationships. By working with a therapist, individuals can gain insight into their own thoughts and behaviors, allowing them to make positive changes in their lives.

Therapy can provide many benefits, including improved self-esteem, better communication skills, and improved relationships. Additionally, therapy can provide tools to manage anxiety, depression, and stress. Further, therapy can help a person to become more aware of their thoughts and emotions, allowing them to process them in a healthier way. Finally, therapy can help to reduce the symptoms of trauma, providing a safe space for the patient to process their experiences.

How therapy can help

Therapy can help individuals by providing an opportunity to explore their thoughts and feelings in a safe, non-judgmental environment. Through treatment, individuals can learn more about themselves, become aware of the patterns and behaviors that are influencing their lives, and gain insight into the causes of their distress. Additionally, therapy can provide tools and strategies to manage stress, anxiety, and other challenging emotions. Therapy can also help individuals to form healthier relationships with themselves and others. Therapy can provide a space for healing from past traumas and develop resilience for future challenges.

Questions to ask before beginning therapy

Before beginning therapy, it is essential to ask yourself a few questions. What do I hope to gain from therapy? What type of therapy would be the best fit for me? What types of issues do I want to address in therapy? What are my expectations for therapy? Am I comfortable talking to a therapist about my feelings and experiences? Do I feel comfortable with the therapist I am considering? Do I have any concerns about the confidentiality of my sessions? Answering these questions can help you determine if therapy is the right step for you.

Tips for making the most of therapy

Making the most of therapy requires effort and commitment. It is important to be open and honest with your therapist. Also, be prepared to discuss complex topics, as this will help you work through issues. Additionally, set realistic goals and objectives for therapy. Make sure to practice what you learn in sessions outside of the office. Finally, trust the therapeutic process and be patient with yourself as you make progress.

Techniques used by the therapist

Therapists will typically use a variety of techniques, depending on the type of therapy they practice. Standard techniques include cognitive-behavioral therapy (CBT), dialectical behavior therapy (DBT), psychodynamic therapy, mindfulness-based approaches, and solution-focused therapy. Each method has its own set of tools and strategies to help individuals work through issues. Your therapist can provide more information on the specific techniques they use in their sessions.

How to ensure a successful outcome

In other to ensure a successful outcome, it is essential to be open and honest with your therapist, set realistic goals, practice what you learn in sessions, and be patient with yourself as you make progress. Additionally, attend all scheduled appointments and be willing to work on the tasks given by your therapist in between sessions. During the therapy process, you can expect to discuss complex topics, learn new strategies for managing stress and emotions, and gain insight into your thoughts and behaviors. With dedication and hard work, therapy can help you make meaningful changes in your life.

What to expect from the therapy process

In the therapy process, you can expect to discuss complex topics, learn new strategies for managing stress and emotions, and gain insight into your thoughts and behaviors. Your therapist will help you identify your goals and create a plan to reach them. Your therapist may also provide education, support, and feedback to help you develop new skills and strategies. During the course of therapy, you should be able to make progress toward your goals and create a better understanding of yourself. It is essential to be open and honest with your therapist and to be patient with yourself as you make progress. It is also necessary to attend all scheduled appointments and be willing to work on the tasks given by your therapist in between sessions. With dedication and hard work, therapy can help you make meaningful changes in your life.

Uncovering the Roots: How Therapy Helps to Get to the Core of Your Problems

When a patient enters therapy, it is essential to remember that they are not just seeking help for the symptom they initially present. Oftentimes, the root of the problem is much deeper than what the patient might think. It is essential to recognize that the patient's problems may be more complex than they initially appear and to take the time to explore and identify underlying issues. This will help the therapist develop a plan of action that can address the issue in its entirety.

When an individual enters therapy, it is often assumed that the problems they are facing are only surface level. However, this assumption is generally untrue. In reality, the issues and struggles that bring individuals to therapy are usually much more profound than first expected. The patient's symptoms may be a result of a much more significant underlying problem that has yet to be uncovered.

Understanding the root of the problem

Understanding the root of the problem is essential in order to develop a practical course of treatment. This can be done through a variety of different therapeutic techniques, such as exploring the patient's history, discussing the patient's current life, and identifying potential underlying issues that are causing distress.

By taking the time to explore the root of the problem, therapists can gain a better understanding of the patient's experiences and how they may be influencing their current state. This allows them to create a plan of action that is tailored to the individual's specific needs and goals.

By uncovering the roots of a patient's issues, therapists can help them gain insight into their struggles, develop healthier coping mechanisms, and ultimately move toward achieving their desired goals. Uncovering the roots is an important step in successful therapy and should not be overlooked. It is essential for therapists to take the time to explore the source of the problem so they can develop an effective treatment plan and help their patients to reach their desired outcomes.

The importance of exploring deeper

Issues in therapy are based on the belief that problems are often rooted in past experiences. By delving into the patient's history and identifying potential underlying problems, therapists can gain a better understanding of the patient's current struggles and create a plan of action that is tailored to their individual needs.

Exploring deeper issues also allows the therapist to create a safe space for the patient to share their thoughts and feelings without fear of judgment or criticism. This helps the therapist to better understand their patient and create an atmosphere of trust and mutual respect.

Exploring deeper issues in therapy can help the patient to gain insight into their own emotions and behaviors, build resilience, increase self-awareness, and develop healthier coping mechanisms. Ultimately, it can help the patient to achieve greater well-being and reach their desired goals.

Analyzing the underlying issue

Allows the patient to gain a better understanding of why they are feeling the way they do and what can be done to improve their situation. By exploring more profound issues, the therapist can help the patient to identify and address the root causes of their distress. This can provide the patient with a greater sense of control over their emotions and behaviors, leading to healthier outcomes.

Furthermore, exploring deeper issues in therapy can help the patient to develop tools that can be used in everyday life. Once underlying problems have been identified and addressed, the patient can begin to develop strategies and skills that will help them to manage their emotions and behaviors in a more effective manner.

Overall, exploring deeper issues in therapy can be an essential part of helping the patient to reach their desired goals and achieve greater well-being. It is necessary for therapists to take the time to listen and understand their patients' experiences so that they can help them to gain insight into the causes of their distress and develop the skills needed for positive change.

Working through the complexities of emotions

And behaviors can be difficult and overwhelming. It is important for therapists to provide a safe, non-judgmental, and confidential environment for the patient to explore their feelings and experiences. By being present and actively listening, the therapist can help the patient to feel heard, understood, and supported. This will, in turn, create a space for deeper exploration, leading to meaningful insight and change.

The therapist can also help the patient to learn how to regulate their emotions and behaviors. This can be done through a variety of techniques, such as mindfulness, cognitive restructuring, and problem-solving. By teaching the patient how to identify and manage their feelings, they can begin to develop healthier coping strategies that will help them to move forward in a more positive direction.

Ultimately, exploring deeper issues in therapy can be an essential part of helping the patient reach their desired goals and achieve greater well-being. By creating a safe and supportive environment, the therapist can help the patient gain insight into the causes of their distress and develop the skills needed for positive change.

Finding the right approach to healing

It is vital to a successful therapy experience. It is important for the therapist to be aware of the patient's needs and to provide a safe and supportive environment for open discussion. However, it is also important for the therapist to help the patient explore deeper issues that may be affecting their mental health. By actively listening and engaging in meaningful conversations, the therapist can help the patient gain insight into their thoughts, feelings, and behaviors, which can lead to meaningful understanding and positive change.

In addition to helping the patient explore their deeper issues, the therapist can also offer various strategies to help the patient cope with their challenges. These strategies can include cognitive-behavioral therapy (CBT) techniques such as relaxation exercises, problem-solving approaches, and cognitive restructuring. Additionally, the therapist can recommend lifestyle changes such as exercise, proper nutrition, and social support. The therapist may also suggest mindfulness techniques, such as meditation and yoga, to help the patient manage stress and cultivate a more positive outlook on life.

Ultimately, these coping strategies can help the patient to move forward in a more positive direction and live a happier and healthier life. By providing a safe and supportive environment for open discussion and exploration of deeper issues, the therapist can help the patient gain insight into the causes of their distress and develop the skills needed for positive change.

How can therapists identify deeper issues in a patient?

Therapists can identify deeper issues in a patient by engaging in an in-depth assessment of the patient's presenting problems. During this assessment, the therapist will ask questions to better understand the patient's background and current circumstances. They may also observe the patient's behavior, language, and body language to gain further insights into their emotional state. Additionally, the therapist may use various psychological tests, such as the MMPI-2 or Rorschach Inkblot Test, to gain additional insight into the patient's mental health. Through this comprehensive assessment process, the therapist can gain a deeper understanding of the patient's experiences, which can then be used to identify underlying issues that are contributing to their distress.

How to address and resolve underlying issues

Once underlying issues are identified, the therapist can help the patient address and resolve these issues by providing therapeutic interventions. For example, the therapist may use cognitive-behavioral therapy (CBT) to help the patient identify and challenge any irrational thoughts and beliefs that are contributing to their distress. Additionally, the therapist may use other forms of therapy, such as psychodynamic therapy, which involves exploring past experiences, or interpersonal therapy, which focuses on improving relationships and communication. Through these interventions, the therapist can help the patient gain insight into the causes of their distress as well as develop the skills needed for positive change.

The importance of considering how the past influences the present

In addition to providing therapeutic interventions, it is essential for the therapist to consider how the patient's past experiences may be influencing their current distress. It is common for people to experience psychological distress as a result of unresolved trauma or past traumas that have not been effectively addressed. By exploring the patient's past experiences, the therapist can gain insight into how these experiences may be influencing the patient's current distress and can then develop an appropriate treatment plan to help the patient address and resolve these issues.

The role of the therapist in helping patients explore deeper issues

The therapist's role is to help the patient identify and explore deeper issues that may be influencing their distress. This may include analyzing the patient's relationships, family history, and own inner thoughts and feelings. Through this process, the therapist can help the patient gain insight into how their experiences have shaped their current situation and can then help them develop the skills needed to make positive changes in their life. Additionally, the therapist can provide support and guidance as the patient works to understand and resolve their issues.

The benefits of tackling underlying issues in therapy

Tackling underlying issues in therapy can provide numerous benefits. It can help patients gain clarity and insight into their current situation, allowing them to develop a better understanding of themselves and their needs. Additionally, it can help them gain the skills needed to address their distress and make positive changes in their life. Finally, it can also help them cultivate more meaningful relationships with those around them. By exploring their issues and providing support and guidance, therapists can help patients build a stronger foundation for their mental health.

Changing the Narrative: How to Challenge Unhelpful Beliefs in Therapy

Everyone experiences problems in life. It is natural to want to make sense of these issues and come up with explanations for why they have occurred. Unfortunately, when we do this, we often develop unhelpful narratives that can contribute to our distress and keep us stuck in unhealthy patterns. This is especially true when it comes to therapy. Patients often come in with a pre-conceived narrative about their issues that can become a barrier to progress.

Fortunately, there are ways to challenge these unhelpful beliefs and narratives. Here are some tips for how to do this in therapy:

1. Identify the Narrative: The first step is to identify the narrative that the patient has created. This can be done through careful listening and questioning. Once the narrative has been identified, it can then be examined for accuracy and helpfulness.

2. Ask Questions: Asking questions about the narrative is a powerful way to challenge it.

These questions should focus on the accuracy of the description as well as how helpful it is in terms of resolving the patient's issues.

3. Explore Alternative Explanations: Encourage the patient to explore alternative explanations for why their issues have occurred. This can help them to see that there are other ways to make sense of their experiences and can help them

What are unhelpful narratives?

Unhelpful narratives are stories or beliefs that people have about themselves and the situations that can prevent them from making progress. These stories can be based on generalizations, negative self-talk, or faulty assumptions. Causes of unhelpful narratives can include negative experiences, trauma, or distorted thinking patterns.

What causes people to have Unhelpful narratives?

Unhelpful narratives can be caused by a variety of factors. These include traumatic or difficult experiences, negative self-talk, and messages from other people that have been internalized. People may also develop unhelpful narratives if they are constantly comparing themselves to others or if they set unrealistic expectations for themselves. It is important to recognize that unhelpful narratives can be modified and replaced with more helpful ones.

How do unhelpful narratives negatively impact people?

Unhelpful narratives can have a negative impact on people by preventing them from making progress and seeking help. They can also cause people to feel hopeless and have low self-esteem, which can lead to depression or other mental health issues. Additionally, unhelpful narratives can cause people to focus on the negative aspects of their lives and ignore the positive ones, which can lead to further feelings of despair.

Strategies to help people challenge and replace unhelpful narratives

1. Encourage people to identify and challenge their unhelpful thoughts: Ask them to be mindful of the stories they tell themselves and to question the evidence that supports those stories.

2. Help people to reframe their thinking: Ask them to look for positive interpretations in situations and to focus on strengths and successes.

3. Model positive self-talk: Encourage people to talk to themselves with kindness and understanding and remind them that mistakes are part of learning and growth.

4. Offer alternative perspectives: Ask people to consider different points of view, including those from other people or from experts in the field.

5. Encourage problem-solving: Ask people to come up with solutions for difficult situations and to practice self-care.

How therapy can help people overcome unhelpful narratives

Therapy can help people to acknowledge, challenge, and replace unhelpful narratives. Through a variety of interventions, such as cognitive-behavioral therapy, solution-focused therapy, and narrative therapy, therapists can help people gain insight into their thoughts and feelings, explore their values and beliefs, and develop new strategies for coping. Therapists can also provide support and guidance as people work to create more positive stories and narratives about themselves.

Introduction to Cognitive Behavioral Therapy (CBT)

Cognitive Behavioral Therapy (CBT) is a form of psychotherapy that focuses on teaching individuals how to recognize and modify their thoughts, emotions, and behaviors in order to better manage difficult situations. CBT emphasizes the importance of examining how our thoughts and beliefs influence our feelings and behaviors. Through the use of techniques such as problem-solving, mindfulness, and cognitive restructuring, people can learn to challenge unhelpful patterns of thinking, manage their emotions more effectively, and take more effective action. CBT can be used to treat a wide range of mental health issues, such as anxiety, depression, substance use disorders, and eating disorders.

How Cognitive Behavioral Therapy (CBT) works

CBT is based on the idea that our thoughts, emotions, and behaviors are all interconnected. When we experience difficult emotions or situations, we may develop patterns of thinking and behaving that are unhelpful or even harmful. CBT teaches us to recognize these patterns so that we can challenge them and replace them with more helpful strategies. In CBT, therapists can help clients learn to identify unhelpful thoughts and create new, more helpful ways of thinking about the situation. Additionally, clients learn skills such as problem-solving and mindfulness to help manage their emotions in healthy ways. Through CBT, individuals can gain a better understanding of themselves and their reactions to difficult situations, enabling them to make changes that lead to improved mental health.

How unhelpful narratives can harm your mental health

Unhelpful narratives are stories and beliefs that we tell ourselves that can be detrimental to our mental health. These narratives can lead to feelings of low self-worth, anxiety, and depression. Examples of unhelpful narratives include: "I'm not good enough," "I don't deserve this," and "I can't do anything right." These narratives can become so ingrained in our thinking that it's difficult to recognize them as unhelpful and to challenge them. However, acknowledging and challenging these unhelpful narratives can be an essential step in improving mental health. CBT can help individuals identify and change these negative thought patterns, allowing them to gain clarity on their thoughts and feelings and create a more positive outlook.

Strategies for reframing negative thoughts and beliefs

Reframing is a cognitive strategy that involves changing the way we think about an event or situation. It can help us to gain perspective and to create new, more helpful narratives. Here are some strategies for reframing unhelpful thoughts and beliefs:

1. Identify unhelpful thoughts: It is important to be aware of the unhelpful thoughts and beliefs that are influencing your mental health. It can be helpful to take a few moments to identify what these thoughts and beliefs are.

2. Challenge the thought: After identifying these thoughts, it can be helpful to challenge them. Ask yourself questions such as "Is this really true?" or "What evidence do I have to support this?" This can help to put the thought in perspective and create a more balanced view.

Reframe the thought: Once you have challenged the idea, it can be helpful to reframe it as something more positive or useful. For example, instead of thinking, "I can't do this," you could reframe it as "I can do this, but I will need support and guidance."

Practice self-compassion: It is essential to be kind to yourself and practice self-compassion. Remind yourself that it is normal to have negative thoughts and feelings at times and that it is ok to make mistakes.

How to create new, helpful narratives

By identifying and challenging unhelpful thoughts and beliefs can be beneficial to create unique, more positive narratives. This could involve writing down positive affirmations or creating a vision board with inspiring images and quotes. It can also be helpful to practice mindfulness and focus on the present moment. Additionally, it can be helpful to practice gratitude and reflect on all the things you are thankful for. Lastly, engaging in activities that bring joy and meaning can help to create a more positive outlook.

Peeling Back the Layers: How Therapists Uncover Patients' Defense Mechanisms

When it comes to psychotherapy, understanding the patient's defense mechanisms is essential to helping them. Defense mechanisms are psychological strategies used by individuals to protect themselves from anxiety, pain, and uncomfortable realities. These mechanisms are unconscious and instinctive and can be detrimental if not addressed. As a therapist, it is important to be able to identify defense mechanisms in order to help the patient work through them.

Introduction: Definition of defense mechanisms

The term "defense mechanisms" was first used by Sigmund Freud in the early 1900s. He defined defense mechanisms as psychological processes that help an individual protect themselves from anxiety or pain. According to Freud, defense mechanisms are unconscious and instinctive and are used to protect the ego from difficult or threatening situations. Many different types of defense mechanisms exist, including denial, repression, displacement, projection, reaction formation, and sublimation.

Step One: Establish Rapport

The first step in understanding a patient's defense mechanisms is to establish a good rapport with them. This means creating a safe and trusting environment for the patient to feel comfortable sharing their thoughts and feelings. A therapist should strive to make their patient feel heard and accepted without judgment.

Step Two: Ask Questions

Once a rapport has been established, the therapist should ask questions in order to gain a better understanding of the patient's defense mechanisms. Questions should focus on the patient's thoughts, feelings, and behavior in various situations. Asking questions about past experiences can also be beneficial in understanding how the patient has responded to difficult situations in the past.

Step Three: Identify Defense Mechanisms

Once the therapist has asked questions and gathered information, they can begin to identify the patient's defense mechanisms. It is important to remember that defense mechanisms can be both positive and negative. For example, denial can be used to protect an individual from facing a difficult reality, while displacement can be used to redirect negative emotions in a healthier way.

Step Four: Help the Patient Work through Defense Mechanisms
Once defense mechanisms have been identified, the therapist

Common Defense Mechanisms Used by Patients

1. Denial: Refusal to accept reality or facts
2. Repression: Pushing away unpleasant thoughts or feelings
3. Regression: Reverting back to immature behavior in order to cope with difficult emotions
4. Projection: Attributing one's own feelings to someone else

5. Displacement: Redirecting negative emotions onto a less threatening target
6. Rationalization: Justifying behaviors or beliefs with logical explanations
7. Sublimation: Channeling negative emotions into socially acceptable activities
8. Reaction Formation: Reacting in the opposite way of one's true feelings
9. Intellectualization: Using logic or analysis to avoid emotionally charged topics
10. Identification: Taking on the personality traits of another person

Peeling Back the Layers: How Therapists Uncover Patients' Defense Mechanisms

When it comes to psychotherapy, understanding the patient's defense mechanisms is essential to helping them. Defense mechanisms are psychological strategies used by individuals to protect themselves from anxiety, pain, and uncomfortable realities. These mechanisms are unconscious and instinctive and can be detrimental if not addressed. As a therapist, it is important to be able to identify defense mechanisms in order to help the patient work through them.

How Patients Use Defense Mechanisms to Avoid Confronting the Truth

Defense mechanisms are unconscious psychological strategies that individuals use to protect themselves from unpleasant emotions and thoughts. In the context of mental health, these mechanisms often arise when patients are faced with information or experiences that challenge their beliefs, values, or self-image.

One common defense mechanism that patients use to avoid confronting the truth is denial. Denial involves refusing to acknowledge a painful or difficult reality, often by pretending it doesn't exist or minimizing its impact. For example, a patient with a serious illness may deny the severity of their condition, insisting that it's just a minor setback that will resolve itself.

Another defense mechanism that patients use to avoid confronting the truth is repression. Repression involves pushing unpleasant memories, thoughts, or emotions out of conscious awareness and into the unconscious mind. This helps the individual avoid facing difficult experiences or feelings that may be too overwhelming to deal with.

Projection is another defense mechanism that patients may use to avoid confronting the truth. Projection involves attributing one's own unacceptable thoughts, feelings, or behaviors to others, often as a way of avoiding responsibility or accountability. For example, a patient with anger issues may project their anger onto others, blaming them for their own feelings of frustration and annoyance.

Rationalization is a defense mechanism that involves offering excuses, justifications, or explanations for behavior that is not in line with one's own values or beliefs. This helps the individual maintain their self-image and avoid facing the truth about their own behavior. For example, a patient who is addicted to drugs may rationalize their use by saying that they only use them to cope with stress or anxiety.

Finally, displacement is a defense mechanism that involves redirecting emotions, impulses, or desires from their original source to a less threatening target. This allows the individual to avoid confronting the truth about their own feelings or behaviors. For example, a patient who is angry with their boss may displace their anger onto a coworker, directing their frustration at someone who is less likely to cause significant harm or consequences.

In conclusion, defense mechanisms are a common way that patients use to avoid confronting the truth. By understanding these mechanisms, mental health professionals can help patients identify and work through their fears and insecurities, allowing them to gain greater insight and understanding into their thoughts, feelings, and behaviors.

How Therapists Can See Through Defense Mechanisms

As a therapist, being able to see through a patient's defense mechanisms is an important part of providing effective treatment. Defense mechanisms are unconscious psychological strategies that individuals use to protect themselves from unpleasant emotions and thoughts. By recognizing and understanding these mechanisms, therapists can help patients gain insight into their behavior and emotions and work towards lasting change and growth.

One key aspect of seeing through defense mechanisms is developing a deep understanding of the patient's personality, history, and motivations. This allows the therapist to recognize when a patient is using a defense mechanism and to identify which specific mechanism is being used. For example, a patient who frequently denies the existence of a problem may be using denial as a defense mechanism.

Another important aspect of seeing through defense mechanisms is maintaining a non-judgmental attitude. Patients who feel judged or criticized are less likely to be forthcoming about their thoughts and feelings, making it harder for the therapist to see through their defense mechanisms. By creating a supportive and understanding environment, therapists can encourage patients to be more open and honest, which can help to reveal their defense mechanisms.

Active listening is another critical aspect of seeing through defense mechanisms. By paying close attention to what a patient is saying and asking open-ended questions that encourage deeper exploration, therapists can help patients to uncover their defense mechanisms and gain a deeper understanding of their underlying emotions and thoughts.

Finally, therapists can use various therapeutic techniques to help patients see through their defense mechanisms. For example, cognitive-behavioral therapy (CBT) can help patients to challenge and reframe negative thoughts, while psychoanalytic therapy can help patients to uncover unconscious thoughts and feelings that are contributing to their defense mechanisms.

In conclusion, seeing through a patient's defense mechanisms is an important part of providing effective therapy. By developing a deep understanding of the patient, maintaining a non-judgmental attitude, actively listening, and using therapeutic techniques, therapists can help patients gain insight into their behavior and emotions and work towards lasting change and growth.

Tips for Therapists to Help Patients Confront the Truth

As a therapist, helping patients confront the truth can be a complex and delicate process. However, it is an essential part of the therapeutic journey and can lead to significant emotional and psychological growth. Here are some tips for therapists to help patients confront the truth:

1. Create a safe and supportive environment: Patients may be afraid to confront the truth if they feel judged or criticized. It's important for therapists to create a non-judgmental and supportive environment where patients feel free to explore their thoughts and feelings without fear of retaliation.

2. Encourage open and honest communication: Encouraging open and honest communication is key to helping patients confront the truth. Therapists can use active listening techniques, such as reflecting back on what they hear and asking open-ended questions, to encourage patients to explore their thoughts and feelings more deeply.

3. Emphasize the benefits of confronting the truth: Patients may resist confronting the truth if they believe it will bring more pain or discomfort. It's important for therapists to emphasize the benefits of facing the truth, such as increased self-awareness, reduced stress, and improved relationships.

4. Use cognitive-behavioral therapy (CBT) techniques: CBT can be an effective tool for helping patients confront the truth. For example, therapists can help patients challenge negative thoughts and beliefs that may be hindering their ability to face reality.

5. Address defense mechanisms: Patients often use defense mechanisms to avoid confronting the truth. It's important for therapists to recognize these mechanisms, such as denial, repression, or projection, and to help patients understand how they are impacting their lives.

6. Be patient and supportive: Confronting the truth can be a difficult and emotional process. Therapists should be patient and supportive, allowing patients to progress

at their own pace and providing encouragement and support along the way.

In conclusion, helping patients confront the truth is an important part of the therapeutic journey. By creating a safe and supportive environment, encouraging open and honest communication, emphasizing the benefits of confronting the truth, using CBT techniques, addressing defense mechanisms, and being patient and supportive, therapists can help patients gain insight into their thoughts and emotions, and work towards lasting change and growth.

Loss as an Integral Part of Change

Loss is a normal part of life, and it's inevitable. We all face losses at some point in our lives. Some are sudden, like the death of a loved one; others are gradual, like the loss of an old job or house; some are expected (like losing your spouse); others aren't even felt until after they've happened--the loss of a friend when they get into an accident on their bike who was riding with them that day and died shortly thereafter.

Loss can be good or bad depending on how you handle it emotionally and mentally, as well as what comes after your loss. If you react with anger toward someone who caused your pain by making insensitive comments about how they should "get over" whatever happened to hurt you so much that you tear up every time someone mentions his name...then yes: this person has done something wrong! It doesn't matter if he meant well or not; all that matters is whether he took responsibility for his actions instead of blaming others for causing his own problems.

Change is a normal and essential part of human growth. Yet people can often stay mired in bad situations because, deep down, they don't want to face the necessary loss that change requires. For example, if a woman discovers that her partner has lied to her, she may downplay this knowledge so that she doesn't have to risk losing the relationship. By avoiding her feelings, she avoids the possibility of loss. But by not facing this potential loss, she remains stuck and unhappy. Change is a part of life. We all experience it in one way or another. It's a natural, if painful, part of being human. Change can be positive and life-changing if you're willing to embrace it, but it also comes with its share of risk and uncertainty. When people experience loss as part of change—when something or someone important to them is taken away from them—they often find themselves grieving over what has been lost and dealing with grief as an integral part of their transition process through change. How to cope with losses Acceptance: Letting go of the past is a difficult task, but it's important to accept your losses and move on. The first step in accepting loss is acknowledging that it has happened—you cannot change what has already occurred. Explore your feelings: This may be difficult if you are feeling angry or upset about losing something dear to you, but try not to let these emotions control your actions or thoughts. Take some time alone to reflect on what happened and how it feels now that it's over; then talk with someone who understands how hard this process can be (such as a friend). Look at the positives: Remembering all the good things about whatever was lost will help put things into perspective so that they don't seem so bad after all (and might even inspire some new ideas!). If there were no negatives associated with losing something like an old picture album full of memories from childhood adventures together as friends, then perhaps getting rid would feel less painful than if there had been negative consequences involved, such as having nothing left behind after moving away from home where everything was crammed into boxes stored away elsewhere until needed again later down the line when needed most. Consider the possibilities: Even if something is no longer available to you, it doesn't mean that there aren't other ways of accomplishing the same goal. If a person or thing was lost, then perhaps you can find someone new who will do just as good a job in their place; if an object was broken, then maybe you can fix it instead of buying a new one (or even better, use it for parts); when something goes missing from view, then it may be because someone else needs it more right now than you do and so they took it away with them to use themselves After a death, there is a grieving process that most people go through. This is normal and healthy and can help you deal with your feelings of loss. The physical symptoms of grief might include headaches, stomach problems, or insomnia; these are all signs that your body is working overtime trying to cope with the pain of your loss. And to help someone else while they are at it. Remember that the world is a big place, and there are lots of people in it who need all kinds of things; sometimes, they just don't know how to get them on their own, so they need someone like you to help out by giving them whatever it is they want (and maybe even more than what they asked for!). Up" what is grieving grief is a natural process. It's normal to feel sad, angry, and even scared at times, but grief reactions can vary widely from person to person. Grieving may take time—but it also takes time away from the loss itself. In most cases, grieving will include both physical and mental aspects: The physical symptoms of grief might include headaches, stomach problems, or insomnia; these are all signs that your body is working overtime trying to cope with the pain of your loss. Mental aspects include sleeplessness or lack of appetite; these feelings may be caused by anxiety about what comes next in your life without the deceased loved one around anymore! If you find yourself feeling guilty about something someone told them during their life (such as cheating), this could also be another symptom of how much they meant to us before you passed away. How to deal with grief and loss? When you lose someone, it's important to remember that grief is a natural process. You cannot stop it from happening, and even if you try to avoid the pain, it will still happen. But what can you do? How do you cope with loss? There are many different ways to deal with grief and loss: talking about it; writing in a journal; calling friends or family members who have been through similar experiences; going to your neighborhood or city (or maybe even country) so that there are no distractions while allowing yourself time alone where thoughts might otherwise creep into your mind at unwanted times throughout the day/night... Why is loss an integral part of the change? Loss is an integral part of the change. Why? Because loss is a part of life. It's something that happens to everyone, and it can feel like you're losing your mind when it happens to you too often or intensely. But if we learn to accept this cycle, then we can live more peacefully in the present moment without focusing on what we've lost or haven't yet gained (which will never be enough). We don't need to try so hard to find happiness; instead, we should focus our energy on finding joy in everything that comes along during each new day—even sadness! Change won't always be easy, but it will be worth it in the end. The change will happen in your life, whether you are ready or not. The good news is that change doesn't mean that everything has to be destroyed and rebuilt from scratch; it just means that things have changed. You can make this journey easier by remembering the following: You don't have to go through all of the pain of change alone, but you do need to be willing to take on whatever comes along with it (and not run away). Change is inevitable and unavoidable—so embrace it as much as possible! Learn to accept that when you lose something, sometimes you gain a part of yourself. Loss is an integral part of the change. It's important to remember that when you lose something, sometimes you gain a part of yourself along with it. When I first moved to New York City, I was very excited about my new job and apartment because they were steps up from living in my parents' basement. But as time passed and more things in life started changing for me—in both positive and negative ways—I realized how much stronger I was becoming as a person because of all the changes that had taken place over the years (and especially since moving away from home). One day while walking down Broadway with my friend Lina, we saw a homeless man sitting on a bench near Washington Square Park begging passersby for money or food scraps out of their pockets (or even just coins). He looked very sad as he stared at us trying not only to attract any attention but also desperately searching for something he could call his own: hope. This image really resonated with me; after all, we're all human beings at heart, so why shouldn't there be room inside each one? Losing something that you love can be devastating, but it is also an integral part of the change. When you lose something, it brings about new opportunities and chances for growth. If, at the end of the day, you feel like there's still room for improvement in your life, then I think that's a sign that there has been some sort of positive change happening within yourself or around you, so keep going with whatever it is we talked about today! :)

The Neutral Zone: Why Therapists Don't Take Sides or Give Advice

We all have an idea of what it's like to go to therapy - a therapist who listens but doesn't judge. One of the most important aspects of a successful therapy session is the therapist's neutrality. We'll discuss what neutrality in therapy is, why it's important, and how to ensure that your therapist remains neutral throughout your session.

What is Neutrality in Therapy?

Neutrality in therapy is the therapist's ability to remain impartial and non-judgmental. It is the therapist's ability to be unbiased and open-minded, to focus solely on the client's needs and goals. Neutrality does not mean that the therapist is indifferent or disconnected - quite the opposite. The therapist must be actively engaged in the session and be able to empathize with the client's feelings and experiences.

The therapist's neutrality allows them to be an effective listener and problem solver. They are able to provide an objective opinion while still respecting the client's autonomy. It also allows the therapist to remain non-confrontational and uninvolved in the client's decisions. Neutrality is a crucial element of the therapeutic relationship, as it helps to build trust and foster positive change.

Benefits of Neutrality in Therapy

Neutrality in therapy has many benefits. Firstly, it allows the therapist to remain impartial and non-judgmental, which helps to create a safe space for the client to explore their thoughts and feelings. It also helps to keep the therapy focused on the client and their needs. The therapist's neutrality encourages the client to take ownership of their own healing and growth.

Moreover, neutrality helps to maintain a trusting relationship between the client and therapist. The client can feel secure in the knowledge that their therapist is not biased and is there to provide a supportive and non-judgmental environment. The therapist's neutrality also allows them to remain objective and provide helpful insights and advice without taking sides or making decisions for the client

Examples of How Therapists Demonstrate Neutrality

There are many ways in which therapists demonstrate neutrality. Firstly, they try to remain objective and non-judgmental in their interactions with the client. They are careful not to make assumptions or offer advice. They also remain open-minded and willing to explore different perspectives and ideas.

In addition, therapists demonstrate neutrality by being respectful and accepting of the client's feelings and experiences. They demonstrate empathy without getting emotionally involved in the situation. They also try to remain unbiased and avoid taking sides or getting caught up in any drama.

How Therapists Use Neutrality to Foster Change

Therapists use their neutrality to help the client explore their thoughts and feelings without judgments or bias. This helps the client to gain insight into their own thoughts and behaviors, which can be a powerful tool for change. It also allows the therapist to help the client identify and address any underlying issues or patterns that may be contributing to the current problem.

The therapist's neutrality also encourages the client to take ownership of their own healing and growth. The client can feel safe in the knowledge that their therapist is not making decisions for them or trying to control the situation. This helps to build trust and foster positive change.

The Importance of Neutrality for Therapists

Neutrality is an essential part of the therapeutic relationship. It helps to create a safe and trusting environment where the client can explore their thoughts and feelings without fear of judgment or criticism. It also helps the therapist to remain objective and provide helpful insights and advice without taking sides or making decisions for the client.

The therapist's neutrality also allows them to remain emotionally connected to the client without becoming emotionally involved in the situation. This helps to ensure that the therapist is able to maintain a professional relationship with the client and provide effective treatment.

How to Ensure Neutrality in Therapy

It is important for therapists to remain neutral in order to provide effective treatment. Here are some tips for ensuring neutrality in therapy:

- Listen actively and attentively: Make sure to focus on the client and their needs rather than getting caught up in your own thoughts or assumptions.

- Remain non-judgmental: Avoid making assumptions or offering advice. Respect the client's autonomy and allow them to make their own decisions.

- Be open-minded: Remain flexible and willing to explore different perspectives and ideas.

- Avoid taking sides: Remain impartial and unbiased in your interactions with the client.

- Maintain a professional relationship: Remain emotionally connected to the client without becoming emotionally involved in the situation.

The Role of Neutrality in Creating Trust in Therapy

The therapist's neutrality is an essential part of creating an atmosphere of trust and safety. The client needs to feel secure in the knowledge that the therapist is not judging them or trying to control the situation. The therapist's neutrality also helps to ensure that the therapy is focused on the client and their needs rather than being distracted by the therapist's own opinions or biases.

The therapist's neutrality is also important for fostering positive change. The client needs to feel comfortable and safe exploring their thoughts and feelings without fear of judgment or criticism. This helps to create an environment where the client can take ownership of their own healing and growth.

The Risks of Taking Sides or Giving Advice in Therapy

Taking sides or giving advice in therapy can have serious consequences. Firstly, it can lead to a breakdown in trust between the client and therapist. The client may feel that the therapist is not listening to them or is trying to control the situation. This can make the client feel invalidated and discouraged, which can impede progress.

In addition, taking sides or giving advice can limit the effectiveness of the therapy. The client may not be able to explore their thoughts and feelings without the fear of judgment or criticism. This can make it difficult for the client to gain insight into their own behavior and make positive changes.

Common Misconceptions about Neutrality in Therapy

There are many misconceptions about neutrality in therapy. Firstly, some people think that neutrality means indifference or disconnection. This is not the case - the therapist must be actively engaged in the session and be able to empathize with the client's feelings and experiences.

Another common misconception is that neutrality means the therapist cannot offer advice or provide insights. This is also not true - the therapist can offer helpful insights and advice without taking sides or making decisions for the client.

Neutrality is an important part of the therapeutic relationship and is essential for providing effective treatment. It helps to create a safe and trusting environment where the client can explore their thoughts and feelings without fear of judgment or criticism. The therapist's neutrality also allows them to provide helpful insights and advice without taking sides or making decisions for the client.

It is important for therapists to ensure that they remain neutral in order to provide effective treatment. This can be done by listening actively and attentively, remaining non-judgmental, being open-minded, avoiding taking sides, and maintaining a professional relationship with the client.

Neutrality is an essential part of the therapeutic relationship and can help to foster positive change in the client.

How the Therapeutic Relationship Can Transform Your Healing Journey

We've all experienced the pain of a broken relationship. Whether it is with a friend, family member, or significant other, it can be hard to find the motivation to start anew. But what if that relationship was with your therapist? Could the therapeutic relationship help heal your wounds and transform your journey to wellness?

The answer is yes, absolutely. A strong therapeutic relationship can be a powerful tool to help you understand and heal from your traumas, anxiety, and depression. In this article, I'll discuss what a therapeutic relationship is, why it's important, and how to build and maintain a successful one.

What is a Therapeutic Relationship?

A therapeutic relationship is a special bond between a therapist and a patient that develops over time. It's based on mutual trust, respect, empathy, and understanding. The therapist listens to the patient, provides support and guidance, and helps the patient to explore emotions and experiences.

This relationship is different from a typical doctor-patient relationship. It's not just about diagnosing and treating a medical condition. It's more of a partnership between two people, where the therapist helps the patient explore and express feelings in a safe and non-judgmental environment.

Why is a Therapeutic Relationship Important?

The therapeutic relationship is the cornerstone of any successful therapy. It's important for several reasons: it helps you to feel safe and comfortable in the therapeutic environment, it builds trust between the therapist and patient, and it allows the therapist to gain a better understanding of the patient's experience.

The therapeutic relationship also helps to create an environment that's conducive to healing. When you feel safe and comfortable, you'll be more likely to open up and explore your feelings. This is essential for healing, as it allows you to gain insight into your emotions, thoughts, and behaviors.

The Phases of a Therapeutic Relationship

The therapeutic relationship typically goes through four distinct phases. These are:

1. Orientation: This is the initial period of the relationship, where the therapist and patient get to know each other and establish a relationship.

2. Working: In this phase, the therapist and patient work together to explore and understand the patient's issues.

3. Termination: This is the final phase of the relationship, where the therapist and patient say goodbye, and the patient is released from therapy.

4. Consolidation: This is the post-therapy phase, where the patient reflects on the experience and integrates it into their life.

What to Expect During Each Phase of the Therapeutic Relationship

During the Orientation phase, you can expect the therapist to ask you questions about your background and history, as well as your goals for therapy. This is a good time for you to get to know the therapist and ask any questions you have about the process.

In the Working phase, the therapist will help you to explore your thoughts and feelings and uncover any underlying issues. This can involve discussing your past experiences, exploring current relationships, and developing strategies for managing difficult emotions.

The Termination phase is a time for the therapist and patient to say goodbye. This can be an emotional experience, but it's also an important part of the healing process. The therapist will help you to process the experience and identify any lasting changes you've made.

Finally, the Consolidation phase is a time for reflection and integration. This is when you can reflect on the experience and the lessons you've learned and integrate them into your life.

Do You Want to Form an Alliance With Me?

One of the most important elements of the therapeutic relationship is the patient-therapist alliance. This is a special bond between the two people that form over time and is essential for successful therapy.

When forming an alliance with your therapist, it's important to be open and honest. Be sure to express your feelings and concerns, and share what you're hoping to get out of the therapy process. This will help your therapist to understand your experience and provide the best possible support.

The Benefits of a Positive Therapeutic Relationship

A positive therapeutic relationship can have a number of benefits. It can help you to feel secure and supported, which can, in turn, help to reduce anxiety and stress. It can also help to reduce the symptoms of depression and allow you to explore your emotions in a safe space.

A positive therapeutic relationship can also help to foster personal growth and development. By exploring your feelings and experiences in a non-judgmental environment, you can gain insight into yourself and develop new strategies for managing difficult situations.

Tips for Developing a Successful Therapeutic Relationship

1. Be open and honest: It's important to be open and honest with your therapist. Express your feelings and concerns, and share what you're hoping to get out of the therapy process.

2. Be patient: The therapeutic relationship takes time to develop. It's important to be patient and give it the time it needs to grow.

3. Ask questions: Don't be afraid to ask questions. This will help you to gain a better understanding of the therapy process and the therapist's approach.

4. Take care of yourself: It's important to take care of yourself both inside and outside of the therapy session. This will help to create a safe and supportive environment.

Building a Safe and Supportive Therapeutic Relationship

In order to build a successful therapeutic relationship, it's important to create a safe and supportive environment. This means creating a space where you feel comfortable and respected and can be yourself without judgment.

One way to do this is to practice self-care. Make sure to take time for yourself and do things that make you feel good. This can include activities such as yoga, meditation, journaling, or spending time with friends and family.

It's also important to be mindful of boundaries. This means respecting the therapist's time, space, and confidentiality. It's important to remember that the therapeutic relationship is professional and not a personal friendship.

Tips for Maintaining a Therapeutic Relationship through Difficult Times

Therapy can be a difficult process, and it's important to maintain a strong therapeutic relationship even through difficult times. Here are some tips for doing so:

1. Talk openly: It's important to talk openly and honestly with your therapist about any difficult feelings or experiences you may be having.

2. Be patient: Mindful that the therapeutic relationship takes time to develop, be patient, and give it the time it needs to grow.

3. Stick to the plan: Don't be discouraged if the therapy process doesn't go as planned. It's important to stick to the plan and stay committed to the process.

4. Ask for help: If you're feeling overwhelmed or like you're not making progress, don't hesitate to ask for help.

Your therapist is there to support you through the process.

A therapeutic relationship is a powerful tool for healing. It can help you to feel safe and supported, explore your emotions, and gain insight into yourself. It's important to create a safe and supportive environment, be open and honest, and practice self-care. With these tips in mind, you can form a successful therapeutic relationship and transform your journey to wellness.

Pain Is Rooted In the Past but Is Associated With Concerns for the Future

We've all had the experience of holding back tears while watching a sad movie. It's a surprisingly powerful demonstration of how much more emotionally painful it is to watch someone else's suffering than our own. But why do we cry more easily when we see other people in pain? Why does watching someone else suffer elicit greater empathetic responses than experiencing our own mental anguish? To answer these questions, let's first examine what causes physical and emotional pain in the first place.

Pain can be a source of suffering, but there is an important distinction between physical pain and emotional pain.

Although physical pain is more immediate and urgent, emotional pain lasts longer than physical. It can be difficult to distinguish between the two because they are often intertwined with each other. Emotional pain is connected to the past, while physical pain is associated with concerns for the future. Physical pains are usually a result of actions or events that have occurred in your life up until now; however, emotional pains usually come from something or someone you experienced in childhood or adolescence (which may have happened years ago).

For example: If you had an accident at work and broke your leg, then this would definitely cause some physical pain, but it wouldn't necessarily bring up any emotions related to past experiences like divorce or abuse by a parent figure.

People tend to view emotional pain as being more harmful than physical pain.

People tend to view emotional pain as being more harmful than physical pain. This is because physical pain can be tied to meaningful events in our past and therefore serve as reminders of the past, whereas emotional pain often occurs when we are reliving a moment from our lives that are connected to an event in our past.

In contrast, people may believe that emotional experiences are transient and not worth dwelling on because they will pass quickly or fade away over time. In this way, feelings associated with emotions like anxiety or sadness may not be considered as threatening or damaging as those related specifically to physical conditions such as arthritis or diabetes--even though both types of problems can cause significant distress for people who experience them.

In addition to these cultural factors, differences between men and women may also play a role in how they cope with emotional pain. Women are more likely than men to experience depression during their lifetimes, and this gender difference may affect how they respond to negative emotions.

Emotional pain can be tied to meaningful events in our past.

Emotional pain can be tied to meaningful events in our past. Emotional pain is associated with negative emotions and a lack of control, predictability, and predictability.

The pain of physical trauma is a biological response to injury or damage to the body. It can be acute (short-term) or chronic (long-term).

Pain is not just an unwelcome sensation; it's also an alarm system that tells us when something is wrong in our bodies.

Pain is not just a symptom of an illness. It can also be a sign that something is wrong with our bodies. It's important to understand the difference between "pain" and "suffering." Pain is simply a sensation in your body; suffering is what you make of it.

We all experience pain at some point in our lives. It can be acute (short-term) or chronic (long-term). Pain is not just an unwelcome sensation; it's also an alarm system that tells us when something is wrong in our bodies. Pain is not just a symptom of an illness. It can also be a sign that something is wrong with our bodies. It's important to understand the difference between "pain" and "suffering." Pain is simply a sensation in your body; suffering is what you make of it.

We often remember emotional events as occurring more vividly than physical events.

We often remember emotional events as occurring more vividly than physical events. For example, when you hear someone tell you they lost their loved one in a car accident, you may feel a pang of sadness but not as much pain or stress.

Emotional memories are also more intense and emotionally laden than physical memories (for example: "I saw my friend who died yesterday").

The advantage of emotional memory is that it gives us insight into our own feelings and experiences--it allows us to see ourselves from another person's point of view by creating empathy for them. On the other hand, this advantage comes at a steep cost: because we're focused on our own feelings, we may not be able to see things objectively or objectively assess what happened during an event itself; instead, we're stuck with only our own perspective!

Physical pain may feel more urgent and pressing than emotional pain.

One of the most common misconceptions about pain is that it's always a physical sensation. While this may be true for some kinds of pain, such as toothaches, other types of discomfort can be emotional in origin. For example, you might feel like your heart is breaking after being rejected by someone close to you or losing a job that was important to you.

Emotional pain is often more intense than physical pain--but it doesn't always feel urgent or pressing on your body. In fact, if you're suffering from an emotional injury, such as feeling hurt because someone broke up with them or lost their job because they weren't good enough at what they did (or both), then there's no doubt that these events have affected them deeply and caused tremendous distress over time; however, those same events might not necessarily cause much actual physical discomfort beyond the initial shock value associated with learning something so upsetting news first hand rather than hearing about it secondhand through social media feeds where everyone seems so happy all the time!

People who are anxious tend to experience greater levels of both physical and emotional pain.

Anxiety is often associated with physical pain. In fact, more than 90 percent of people who experience severe anxiety also report experiencing physical discomfort. This is because the stress response has a number of physiological effects on the body that can lead to chronic pain conditions such as headaches and backaches.

In addition to causing physical symptoms, anxiety also seems to increase your risk of developing depression in the future--the same way it increases your risk of developing other mental health conditions like bipolar disorder or schizophrenia (if you're especially vulnerable).

Overthinking about the future (i.e., worry) increases both physical and emotional pain at the same time because it amplifies each type of hurt separately, making them more painful than they would normally be in isolation from each other.

Overthinking about the future (i.e., worry) increases both physical and emotional pain at the same time because it amplifies each type of hurt separately, making them more painful than they would normally be in isolation from each other.

If you think about your future self as a separate person from yourself right now, then overthinking will make you feel worse about your current condition--a vicious cycle that can compound into a dangerous spiral of self-doubt and guilt.

We know that the world is full of pain, but we can choose to be aware of where our own fears come from. This awareness will help you see when your thoughts are causing pain and take steps to avoid those situations or outcomes. We can also choose to be more forgiving of ourselves and of others. We are all human, and we all make mistakes. When you find yourself hurting, try to remember that it's not your fault--and neither is it anyone else's.

How self-sabotage can be an illusion of control

Self-sabotage is a behavior pattern that can be seen in many people. It is a way of exerting control over one's life and circumstances, even when the outcome may not be favorable. Self-sabotage can take many forms, from procrastinating on important tasks to avoiding challenging conversations to self-medicating with drugs or alcohol. It is a way of trying to control the uncontrollable and protect oneself from potential hurt or disappointment. While self-sabotage can lead to negative outcomes, it is important to remember that it can also be a way of coping with difficult situations. By understanding why you might be engaging in self-sabotaging behavior, you can begin to take steps toward making positive changes in your life.

Self-sabotage is a common behavior that many people engage in without realizing it. It is a form of self-sabotage in which one consciously or unconsciously takes actions that are contrary to what one wants to achieve. Self-sabotaging behaviors can be seen in many aspects of life, including relationships, careers, and health. Self-sabotage can be used as a way to control situations or people. When someone is afraid to take a risk or step out of their comfort zone, they may self-sabotage in order to stay in their comfort zone. Alternatively, when someone is afraid of failure or success, they may self-sabotage to avoid either outcome. Self-sabotage can also be a form of control when used to manipulate people or situations. For example, a person may sabotage their own efforts or relationships.

Self-sabotage is a form of control. It is a way of trying to control outcomes, situations, and relationships in your life. Self-sabotage can take many forms; procrastination, perfectionism, negative self-talk, avoidance, and more. It is a way to try to control the unpredictable and uncertain aspects of life. At its core, self-sabotage is a way to manage fear. Fear of failure, fear of success, fear of the unknown, fear of being judged, fear of losing control - all of these fears can lead us to self-sabotage in an attempt to keep us safe.

The role of fear in self-sabotage cannot be overstated.

Fear is often the underlying cause of self-sabotage. When we are afraid of failure, success, or the unknown, we resort to self-sabotage as a way to protect ourselves. Self-sabotage can become a habit, and it can be difficult to break. The good news is that with awareness and effort, it can be done. Acknowledging and understanding our fears is the first step in overcoming self-sabotage. Once we have identified our fear, we can create strategies to address it and work towards our goals. It may be helpful to seek support from a counselor, psychologist, or support group to help us understand our fears and develop strategies to manage them.

Why we choose to self-sabotage can be complex, but it is often rooted in fear.

Fear of failure, fear of success, fear of the unknown – all of these can lead us to self-sabotage as a way to protect ourselves from the risks associated with these fears. Self-sabotage can become a habit, and it can be difficult to break. Recognizing the fear behind our self-sabotaging behaviors and creating strategies to address it is key to overcoming self-sabotage and working towards our goals.

Recognizing when we are self-sabotaging.

This can be difficult, but it is important to be aware of our thoughts and feelings, as well as our behaviors.

Ask yourself if what you are doing is helping you achieve your goals or if it is holding you back. If you recognize that you are self-sabotaging, the next step is to identify the underlying fear that is driving this behavior. Once you have identified your fear, you can create strategies to address it and work towards your goals. It may be helpful to seek support from a counselor, psychologist, or support group to help you understand your fears and develop strategies to manage them. With awareness and effort, it is possible to break the habit of self-sabotage and work towards achieving your goals.

The consequences of self-sabotage can be Damaging, but with awareness and effort, possible to break the habit of self-sabotage and work towards your goals.

Recognizing the fear behind our self-sabotaging behaviors and creating strategies to address it is key to overcoming self-sabotage. Seeking support from a counselor, psychologist, or support group can help you understand your fears and develop strategies to manage them. With the right support and determination, you can break the cycle of self-sabotage and start working towards your goals.

Strategies for overcoming self-sabotage include identifying the fear behind your self-sabotaging behavior and developing strategies to address it.
It may be helpful to seek support from a counselor, psychologist, or support group to help you understand your fears and develop strategies to manage them. Additionally, creating a plan of action and setting realistic goals can help you stay on track and move closer to achieving your goals. Finally, cultivating self-compassion and understanding that mistakes are a part of the growth can help you stay motivated and break

the cycle of self-sabotage. With the right strategies, it is possible to break the habit of self-sabotage and work towards achieving your goals.